REAL ESTATE RICHES

The unlocking of the codes to
successful investments

Michael Lawson

Preface

I'm glad you're reading "Real Estate Riches: The Unlocking of the Codes to Successful Investments." In writing this book, I've made it my duty to impart to you the knowledge, insights, and tactics that have stoked my enthusiasm for real estate investing and improved my experience in this exciting industry.

Since I was a little child, real estate has mesmerized me with its limitless possibilities and potential for financial gain. My family has a long history in the real estate business, and it was thanks to them that I learned about the transforming impact of smart financial decisions. I have had the opportunity to experience the highs and lows of the market, the excitement of profitable endeavors, and the priceless lessons gained through obstacles encountered along the way.

My commitment to real estate investing extends beyond a desire for financial gain. It is motivated by a sincere desire to enable others to follow this fruitful path and leave a legacy of financial success.In order to provide a thorough manual that will serve as a knowledge resource for both beginning and experienced investors, I have condensed the wisdom I've gathered over the course of many years of experience into this book.

You will begin on a trip through these pages that will provide you with the tools necessary to negotiate the complexity of the real estate market. Each chapter is designed to provide you with practical advice, from comprehending market trends and important drivers to monitoring financial measures and minimizing risks.

In "Real Estate Riches," I place a strong emphasis on the necessity of changing with the times, spotting new opportunities, and making wise choices. I think that a mix of foresight, research, and a dedication to excellence is the key to successful investing.

I urge you to approach this book with an open mind, a thirst for knowledge, and a commitment to put the ideas presented into practice as you read the chapters that lie ahead. By the time we're done, I hope you'll be motivated to move forward with your real estate investing plans with renewed confidence.

I want to express my sincere gratitude to everyone who helped me with this project, from family and friends to other real estate aficionados. Your support and conviction in my objective have served as a constant source of inspiration.

I hope your real estate endeavors are successful. As you unlock real estate's limitless potential and pave the route to prosperity, may "Real Estate Riches: The unlocking of the codes to successful investments" serve as your compass.

- Michael Lawson

Acknowledgment

Writing "Real Estate Riches: The Unlocking of the Codes to Successful Investments" has been a labor of love and devotion on my part, and it would be wrong of me not to offer my sincere gratitude to those who have encouraged and supported me along the way.

I will always be grateful to my family for igniting my passion for real estate at a young age and for their continuous support in all of my endeavors. Your advice and support have been the foundation of my path.

I want to express my gratitude to my real estate sector friends and colleagues for your wisdom, support, and common experiences. Your contributions have improved this book and strengthened my faith in the merits of teamwork.

I appreciate you picking "Real Estate Riches" as your road map to success, readers, whether you are an established investor or an aspiring business owner. It is my genuine wish that the information provided on these pages will encourage and equip you to reach your financial objectives.

I owe a debt of gratitude to the teachers and mentors who helped me develop a grasp of real estate investing. Your guidance and teachings had a lasting impression on my path and served as the basis for this book.

I'm humbled and appreciative to the readers who shared their experiences and stories. Your eagerness to develop together with me has been a fantastic inspiration.

Last but not least, I want to express my sincere gratitude to my editor and proofreaders, whose keen observation and attention to detail made sure that this book was at its best.

Thank you to everyone who helped make this project a success and helped me on my quest to realizing "Real Estate Riches." Together, we crack the codes to success and open the door to a prosperous future.

With gratitude and anticipation,

Michael Lawson

Contents

6. Chapter 6: Adapting to Market Changes and Real Estate Cycles

Introduction

Greetings from the enthralling world of real estate investing, where chances abound and the potential for financial success is limitless. In "Real Estate Riches: The Unlocking of the Codes to Successful Investments," I, Michael Lawson, invite you on a transformative journey that will forever shift your perspective of real estate and equip you with the information and tactics to unlock your route to riches.

I have spent more than 20 years immersed in the dynamic world of real estate, learning how to navigate market changes, take advantage of new possibilities, and hone my skills as an investor and subject matter expert. Because of my family's history in the field, I developed a passion for real estate from a young age. Over the years, I have seen directly how real estate can lead to financial freedom and the transformational potential of wise investing.

This book's goal is to impart to you the secrets of real estate investing success. This book is intended to be your thorough guide, whether you are an ambitious investor eager to take your first steps or a seasoned professional looking to improve your strategy. In these pages, I will demystify the complexity of the real estate market, decipher the secrets of profitable investments, and give you the tools you need to successfully negotiate the ever-evolving terrain of the business.

Firstly We shall set out on a mission to comprehend the real estate market. I'll explain its main forces, a variety of investment options, and techniques for analyzing market trends and potential hazards. With this information at your disposal, you will be better equipped to choose investments that will help you achieve your financial objectives.

Focus once more on developing a sound investing plan that represents your financial capacity and risk tolerance. While appreciating the relevance of diversification and portfolio management, I will emphasize the importance of defining clear investment goals and objectives.

Additionally, we'll go into the field of financial analysis to provide you the tools you need to accurately assess possible properties. I'll walk you through important measures like cash flow, cap rates, and ROI while utilizing financial instruments to help you choose wise investments.

In Chapter 4, as we discuss the legal and regulatory components of real estate investing, I will inform you of key legal principles, tax ramifications, and due diligence. You may protect your investments for long-term success by avoiding legal hazards and maximizing tax methods.

The need for efficient property management and maintenance will be discussed in Chapter 5. To ensure long-term profitability, I will emphasize the value of cultivating good tenant relationships, picking reputable property managers, and putting in place cost-effective maintenance procedures.

Lastly, Chapter 6 will provide you with the skills necessary to adjust to market shifts and profit from upswings. We will look into the real estate market's cyclical nature, discovering new opportunities and risk-reduction tactics for times when the market is weak.

My goal in writing this book is to arm you with the knowledge and direction you need to fully realize the enormous potential of real estate investing. Each chapter is painstakingly written to provide you with practical advice and calculated steps to pave your road to success.

As we open the doors to real estate wealth together, I cordially welcome you to join me on this revolutionary journey and embrace the secrets of wise investing. Let's continue our adventure, learning the tricks of the real estate trade and exploring the seemingly endless opportunities that lie ahead.

We're glad you're here at "Real Estate Riches: The Unlocking of the Codes to Successful Investments." One property at a time, we will work together to create a legacy of success and prosperity.

- Michael Lawson

Chapter 1

Understanding the Real Estate Market

In this foundational chapter, we dive deep into the intricacies of the real estate market, unraveling its complexities and shedding light on essential factors that drive its dynamics.

An overview of the real estate market and its key drivers

The real estate market includes a broad and varied panorama of properties, ranging from houses and flats for living to businesses, factories, and undeveloped land. Demand and supply combine in this dynamic environment to produce opportunities for landlords, investors, and tenants alike.

The idea of property ownership and use is at the center of the real estate industry. Properties are tangible assets that give people and businesses a place to live, a place to work, or commercial space. To comprehend how the market operates, it is essential to comprehend how these attributes interact.

Key Drivers of the Real Estate Market:

1. **Population and Demographics**: Population changes and demographics have a significant impact on the real estate market. As cities expand, there is a greater need for infrastructure, commercial space, and housing, which has an impact on the cost of real estate and rental rates. Investors might find new opportunities in regions with prospective growth by analyzing demographic changes and population shifts.

2. **Economic Factors**: The situation of the economy has a big impact on the real

estate market. Demand and price trends for real estate are influenced by variables including GDP growth, employment rates, and consumer confidence. A healthy economy typically results in higher demand for residential and commercial real estate, which raises property values.

3. **Interest Rates and Mortgage Accessibility**: The affordability of real estate investments is directly impacted by interest rates. Lower interest rates stimulate borrowing, which boosts demand and drives up the price of real estate. Furthermore, simple access to mortgage loans can encourage property purchases and influence the mood of the market as a whole.

4. **Dynamics of Supply and Demand**: Just like any market, the real estate industry runs on the idea of supply and demand. Property prices are influenced by imbalances between the amount of available homes and the number of prospective buyers or tenants. For making strategic investment decisions, it is

essential to comprehend local supply and demand dynamics.

5. Government Policies and laws: The real estate market may be greatly impacted by government policies and laws. Building codes, tax breaks, and zoning regulations all define the kinds of developments that are permitted and have an impact on property values. Understanding the regulatory environment enables investors to avoid risks and take advantage of opportunities.

6. Infrastructure and Development: A location's appeal is increased by the presence of strong infrastructure, such as transportation systems, educational institutions, medical facilities, and amenities. Infrastructure-developed areas typically draw greater investment and see sustained increases in property values.

Understanding these fundamental forces will help you better understand how the real estate market functions and the variables that affect its success.

Understanding these essentials will serve as the cornerstone for making wise and fruitful real estate investment decisions, regardless of your level of experience or where you are in your investing career. So let's explore the fascinating opportunities that the real estate industry presents.

Exploring different types of properties and investment opportunities

The many sorts of properties and investment options that are accessible within the diverse real estate market will be explored in this section.

1. **Residential Properties**: In the real estate market, residential properties are arguably the most well-known and sought-after assets. They include apartment complexes, townhomes, condominiums, and single-family homes. With these properties, investors have a variety of

possibilities, from purchasing a property for personal use to becoming a landlord and earning rental income.

- Single-Family Homes: These properties offer solitude and the chance for long-term appreciation, making them ideal for investors looking for consistent rental income or homeownership.

- Multi-Unit Properties: Duplexes, triplexes, and apartment buildings give investors looking for increased cash flow potential the chance to create numerous rental incomes from a single investment.

2. **Commercial Properties**: Businesses are catered to by commercial properties, which provide a wide range of investment opportunities for individuals seeking diversification and higher profits. Offices, retail establishments, warehouses, and industrial facilities are all part of the commercial sector.

- Office Spaces: Investing in office buildings can be profitable, especially in busy cities where firms are in great demand for centralized sites.

- Retail Spaces: Opportunities to profit from consumer spending and thriving retail marketplaces are provided by retail properties, which range from shopping malls to standalone stores.

- Industrial Facilities: Logistics firms are vying for warehouses and distribution centers, opening up intriguing investment prospects in the expanding e-commerce sector.

3. **Land**: Investing in undeveloped land is a popularly disregarded but effective real estate market tactic. For patient investors, raw land is a desirable option since it has the possibility for development or appreciation.

- Development Land: Those with an eye toward future growth and development can buy land in developing areas, assuring the possibility of a considerable increase in value as the area develops.

- Farmland: When farmland is leased to farmers, it can provide reliable returns, and depending on the state of the agricultural market, its value may rise.

4. **Real Estate Investment Trusts (REITs)**: REITs are a great option for people looking for a less involved real estate investment strategy. Investors can purchase shares of REITs on the stock market, and these publicly traded businesses own and manage properties that generate revenue.

Equity REITs: These REITs are largely engaged in the ownership and management of properties that generate revenue, such as residences, offices, and retail establishments.

- Mortgage REITs: With a focus on offering funding for real estate deals, mortgage REITs make money by charging interest on mortgage loans.

5. **Real Estate Partnerships and Syndications**: Investors can pool their funds through partnerships and syndications to take part in bigger and more successful real estate ventures. These chances can provide diversification and access to business ventures that could be beyond the price range of individual investors.

A universe of opportunities becomes available when looking into these different kinds of properties and investment prospects. As you move forward in your real estate career, keep in mind to match your investing decisions to your own preferences, risk tolerance, and financial objectives. We've built the groundwork; let's go on and investigate the fascinating world of real estate investment.

Analyzing market trends and potential risks

In this section, we'll go into detail about how important it is to assess market trends and spot potential hazards in the always changing real estate market. By learning this ability, you'll have the knowledge you need to make wise and calculated financial choices.

1. **Market investigation and data analysis**: The basis for effective real estate investing is rigorous market research. To acquire information on real estate sales, rental rates, and market trends, turn to trustworthy sources like your neighborhood real estate associations, government publications, and respected web directories.

- Understanding patterns and spotting possibilities requires data analysis. To identify places with growth potential or undervalued assets, compare property values in various neighborhoods and analyze historical trends.

2. **Supply and Demand Dynamics**: Assessing market performance requires an understanding of the equilibrium between

supply and demand. While an undersupply of homes might cause prices to rise, an oversupply can result in lower prices and lower rental revenue.

- Keep a watch on population growth, job rates, and demographic changes because these factors directly affect the demand for housing.

3. **Economic Indicators**: The real estate market is greatly influenced by economic indicators including GDP growth, unemployment rates, and consumer confidence. A healthy economy typically results in more demand for and appreciation of real estate.

- To foresee potential effects on the real estate market, keep up with regional and worldwide economic developments.
6. Geographical and location-specific considerations: The appeal and potential value of a property are significantly influenced by its location. Property values can be strongly impacted by variables like

proximity to services, employment areas, schools, and transit hubs.

- Do your homework on the areas you're interested in, taking into account things like crime statistics, infrastructure advancements, and upcoming developments.

Potential Risks:

1. **Market turbulence**: Real estate markets are susceptible to cyclical turbulence. Economic downturns, shifts in demand, or oversupply are just a few examples of reasons that might cause changes in property values.

2. **Economic Downturns**: A downturn in the economy can lower demand for real estate and rental rates, which can have an impact on cash flow and property values.

3. **Interest Rate Changes**: - Increasing mortgage expenses due to rising interest

rates may make homes less affordable for buyers and reduce demand for real estate.

4. **Risks peculiar to a particular property**: Each property has a specific set of risks, such as structural problems, environmental dangers, or title difficulties. To reduce these risks, carry out thorough inspections and due diligence.

5. **Legal and Regulatory Risks**: Modifications to laws and regulations may have an effect on property values, tenancy rules, and the viability of an investment as a whole.

6. **Natural disasters and climate hazards**: Homes in locations vulnerable to natural catastrophes, including floods or earthquakes, entail increased risks that could lower property values and increase insurance costs.

You may better manage the complex world of real estate investment by carefully examining market trends and spotting potential dangers. Take in the information you learn, and never forget that making strategic decisions is the key to developing a profitable and durable real estate portfolio. Let's continue our exploration and learn how to get rich in real estate.

Chapter 2

Creating a Solid Investment Strategy

Setting clear investment goals and objectives

A successful real estate investing strategy must start with well defined investment goals and objectives. Well-defined objectives provide your investing journey direction, focus, and motivation. Let's look at the significance of having specific investment goals and how to achieve it well:

1. **Clarity and Concentration**: Clear investment objectives provide you a target to shoot towards and help you keep focused on your objectives. Having a clearly defined goal helps you stay on track whether you're trying to earn passive income, pay for

retirement, or accumulate long-term wealth.

2. **Measuring and Monitoring Progress**: Setting definite, quantifiable objectives enables you to monitor your development and gauge your performance. You can find areas for growth and recognize achievements by regularly examining your accomplishments in relation to these goals.

3. **Management of Risk**: Knowing your investment objectives enables you to match your strategies and risk tolerance. The kinds of properties you look at and the span of your investing horizon will depend on how much risk you're ready to take on.

4. **Decision-Making**: Your decision-making is influenced by having defined goals. It becomes simpler to examine whether proposed investments are in line with your goals and overarching strategy.

5. **Planning for the future**: An investment with long-term effects is real estate. You can prepare for the future and

make decisions that support your financial vision when your goals are well established.

Tips for Setting Clear Investment Goals

1. Be Specific: Clearly state your objectives. Specify the precise results you intend to attain and stay away from generalizations.

2. Make Goals Measurable: Establish quantitative benchmarks to evaluate development and achievement. For instance, decide how many homes you want to buy or how much rental money you want to bring in each year.

3. Set Achievable Goals: While it's important to have great dreams, make sure your objectives are doable. Unfounded hopes can cause annoyance and disappointment.

4. Establish a Timeline: Create a schedule for completing your objectives. A specific

deadline instills a sense of urgency and aids in helping you prioritize your efforts.

5. Put Your Goals in Writing: Writing down your goals helps you stay committed to them and acts as a regular reminder of your aspirations.

6. Review and Modify: Regularly assess your objectives and modify them as necessary. Your investing strategy may need to be modified as a result of shifting market conditions and life circumstances.

Always keep in mind that the key to a successful real estate investment journey is defining clear investment goals. Consider your goals in light of your risk tolerance, evaluate your financial situation, and reflect on your desires. You'll be more equipped to make wise choices and realize your real estate investment goals if you have a clear road map in place. Let's move forward and design a path to real estate wealth.

Developing a personalized investment strategy based on risk tolerance and financial capacity

Successful real estate investing involves creating a customized investment plan based on your risk tolerance and financial resources. This personalized method guarantees that your investment choices reflect your degree of tolerance with risk as well as your capacity for funding and managing your assets. Let's look at how to design a tailored plan for your particular situation:

1. **Determine Your Risk Tolerance**: Analyze your level of comfort with taking on financial risk. Real estate investments can be low-risk, reliable options or high-risk, lucrative ones.

- Take into account elements including your age, financial objectives, and previous investing experience. While investors who are closer to retirement may place a larger priority on consistent cash flow and lesser volatility, younger investors with longer time horizons might be more inclined to take on higher risk.

- To guarantee that the decisions you make are in line with your comfort zone, be honest with yourself about your risk tolerance.

2. **Identify Your Financial Capacity**: Assess your financial condition to ascertain how much money you can set aside for real estate investments without jeopardizing your long-term financial security.

- Keep in mind elements like your current income, savings, outstanding debt, and spending. Calculate how much of your available cash you can put toward investing without compromising your standard of living or your emergency fund.

To prevent overextending yourself and to choose investments responsibly, it's vital to have a clear grasp of your financial capabilities.

3. **Pick an Investment Strategy**: - Select the best investment strategy based on your risk tolerance and financial resources. This could range from more cautious buy-and-hold tactics to active, possibly riskier, options.

- A cautious approach: Choose reliable, income-producing assets with an eye toward long-term growth. This strategy provides consistent cash flow and the possibility of long-term appreciation.

- Aggressive Approach: Go after higher-risk, higher-reward tactics, including development or fix-and-flip projects. This strategy may involve making short-term investments, and it calls for a readiness to deal with market turbulence and probable setbacks.

4. Diversify Your Portfolio: Diversification is essential regardless of your risk tolerance or financial resources. To reduce risks and improve the performance of your portfolio as a whole, diversify your assets over a range of property kinds and geographical regions.

- Diversifying your portfolio offers protection from market volatility and helps balance the possible drawbacks of specific assets.

5. Stay Informed and Flexible: - Stay up to date on market developments, financial situations, and legislative changes. Because the real estate market is fluid, being adaptive lets you change your approach as necessary.

- Continue to learn about real estate investing, and when required, seek out expert guidance.

You position yourself for long-term success in real estate by creating a customized investment plan based on your risk tolerance and financial capability. Accept your special situation, keep your eye on your objectives, and think carefully before making each investment. Let's move on with assurance and maximize your unique real estate investment path.

Understanding the importance of diversification and portfolio management

To achieve a balanced and durable real estate investment strategy, it is essential to comprehend the value of diversification and portfolio management. These procedures lay the groundwork for long-term success by minimizing risks, maximizing returns, and maximizing returns. Let's examine why portfolio management and diversification are essential in real estate investing:

1. **Reducing Risk**: By diversifying your investments, you can spread your risk over a variety of real estate kinds and geographical regions. By doing this, you

lessen the effect that the performance of any one investment will have on your portfolio as a whole.

- Other investments may be able to offset losses from underperforming assets or market segments, lowering overall risk exposure.

2. **Improving Returns**: - Diversification enables you to access a range of real estate markets and property kinds that might go through multiple growth cycles. By capturing possible gains from several sources, this could raise overall returns.

- A diversified portfolio with a mix of reliable income-producing real estate and higher-yield, growth-oriented investments can produce both cash flow and long-term value.

3. **Adaptability to Market Fluctuations**: Real estate markets occasionally go through cycles of expansion, stability, and decline. Because it is less dependent on the success of a single

market or asset, a diversified portfolio is better able to withstand market swings.

- Income-producing properties may offer stability during economic downturns, while growth-oriented assets may recoup when the market swings around.

4. **Adaptability to Changing Conditions**: Your investment objectives may be affected by alterations in both market conditions and personal circumstances. Flexibility is provided by a varied portfolio, which enables you to modify your plan without fully changing your approach to investing.

- A diverse portfolio gives you the flexibility to alter when your risk tolerance or financial capacity vary over time, all the while remaining within your comfort range.

5. **Managing Cash Flow**: Diversification might assist in balancing the cash flow among your investments. Properties with stable rental income can compensate for

those with erratic cash flow patterns by generating a steady stream of income.

6. **Active Portfolio Management**: It's crucial to consistently track and manage your portfolio. Review market conditions, evaluate each investment's performance, and base your decisions on your investment objectives.

- Portfolio management guarantees that your investments are in line with your level of risk tolerance and your financial goals. Additionally, it enables you to spot chances to profit from market trends and make any necessary strategic adjustments.

In constructing a durable and effective real estate investment plan, diversification and portfolio management are crucial. Spreading risk, increasing profits, and adapting to shifting market dynamics are all benefits of diversification. Maintain market awareness, regularly examine and tweak your portfolio, and be ready to capture opportunities that support your long-term goals. You may fully realize the potential of your real estate wealth by comprehending and putting these strategies into effect.

Chapter 3

Mastering Financial Analysis for Real Estate

Learning how to perform a thorough financial analysis of potential properties

An important stage in real estate investment is doing a comprehensive financial study of possible properties. It aids in your evaluation of the prospective revenue, costs, and overall profitability of the asset. Here is a step-by-step tutorial for learning how to conduct financial analysis:

1. **Gather Important Property Information**: Begin by compiling pertinent property data, such as the asking price, square footage, number of units (if

applicable), and any other features or amenities.

2. **Assess Rental revenue**: - Investigate comparable homes in the neighborhood to ascertain the property's prospective rental revenue. Based on the condition of the property and any special features, consider the typical rent for units that are comparable to it.

3. **Calculate Gross Income**: - Multiply the estimated rental income by the number of units (if appropriate) to arrive at the gross income. You will then know the entire income the property has produced.

4. **Estimate Operating Expenses**: - List and calculate all ongoing expenditures associated with maintaining the property, such as utilities, maintenance bills, insurance, taxes, and property management fees.

5. **Calculate Net Operating Income (NOI)**: - To calculate Net Operating Income (NOI), subtract the gross income

from all operating expenditures. After all running expenses are subtracted, NOI shows the property's income.

6. Examine Cash Flow: Cash flow is an important aspect of real estate investing. Subtract the monthly cash flow from the NOI along with any applicable mortgage payments and other non-operating costs.

 - A positive cash flow shows that the property makes more money than it spends, giving you a steady stream of revenue.

7. Take Financing Costs into Account: If you intend to use a mortgage to finance the property, consider the mortgage interest, loan terms, and down payment to determine how they will affect your cash flow and overall return on investment.

8. Determine the Potential for Appreciation: While financial analysis concentrates on short-term gains, take into account the property's potential for long-term growth. To determine the property's long-term value, research market trends, local developments, and growth estimates.

9. Calculate ROI (Return on Investment): - Divide the property's net profit (cash flow) by your initial investment (down payment and closing costs) to determine the Return on Investment (ROI). A high ROI denotes a successful investment.

10. Perform a sensitivity analysis: Analyze sensitivity by simulating various circumstances. Analyze the effects of variations in expenses, rental income, or interest rates on the property's financial performance.

11. Compare with Other Properties: Examine the financial analysis' findings against those of nearby properties that are comparable. This assists you in identifying the best investing options and helping you make informed judgments.

Remember that making wise investing selections requires completing a thorough financial analysis. Take your time, collect reliable information, and make realistic estimates. Your ability to assess possible properties will improve with time and experience, raising your likelihood of real estate investing success. Let's hone our abilities in financial analysis and find the key to real estate wealth.

Evaluating key metrics like cash flow, cap rates, and ROI

In real estate investing, it is essential to assess important parameters like cash flow, cap rates, and ROI. These statistics offer insightful information about the property's profitability and possible return on investment. Let's investigate how to assess these crucial metrics:

1. **Cash flow**: Cash flow is the property's net income after all operating costs and mortgage payments (if any) have been subtracted. Positive cash flow means the

property makes more money than it spends, giving you consistent revenue.

- To determine cash flow, deduct the property's gross income, or Net Operating Income (NOI), from all operating costs and mortgage payments.

- A positive cash flow makes sure you have enough money to pay for expenses, maintenance, and unforeseen charges while making a profit.

2. **Cap Rate (Capitalization Rate)**: A key indicator of a property's prospective return on investment is the cap rate. Based on the property's Net Operating Income (NOI) and current market value, it shows the rate of return for the asset.

- Divide the property's NOI by its current market value, then multiply the result by 100 to indicate the cap rate as a percentage.

- Cap rates change depending on the market, the type of property, and the region. Though it's important to take the larger market environment into account, greater cap rates typically signal higher potential gains.

3. **Return on Investment (ROI)**: ROI gauges how profitable an investment is in comparison to its price. It displays the % return on your initial investment that you might anticipate.

- To calculate return on investment (ROI), divide the cash flow from the property's net profit by the whole amount you invested (down payment and closing costs), then multiply the result by 100 to get the ROI as a percentage.

- A positive ROI shows that your investment is lucrative, whereas a negative ROI shows that it isn't bringing in enough money.

4. **Things to Think About When Assessing Metrics**:
- Context Matters: Think about the measurements in light of the particular property, location, and market

circumstances. What can be considered a high or low cap rate in one market might not apply in another.

- Long-Term Perspective: While cash flow and cap rates offer insights into immediate returns, think about the property's long-term appreciation potential and overall investment goals.

- Sensitivity Analysis: Perform a sensitivity analysis to see how adjustments to expenses, interest rates, or rental income may affect cash flow, cap rates, and ROI.

- Compare to Similar Properties: In order to find the best investment options, compare the metrics with those of nearby properties that are similar to your own.

You can choose investments wisely and find properties that fit your financial goals by analyzing important parameters like cash flow, cap rates, and ROI. These measurements offer a numerical framework for evaluating the property's financial performance and its potential to be a successful investment. Let's move on with assurance and discover the road to real estate wealth.

Using financial tools and software to aid in decision-making

Real estate investment decision-making can be greatly aided by the use of financial tools and software since they offer data-driven insights, streamline analysis procedures, and help in modeling various scenarios. The following are some ways that financial software and tools can facilitate decision-making:

1. **Property Analysis**: Financial tools can perform thorough property analyses, accurately and precisely determining important parameters including cash flow, cap rates, and ROI.

- They can evaluate the property's potential for income, running costs, and financing costs to give a clear picture of its financial health.

2. **Market Data and Trends**: Financial software has real-time access to market data and trends, which can help you keep up with changes in real estate prices, tenancy rates, and economic indicators.

- Understanding market trends enables you to make judgments that are well-informed by the situation at hand as well as prospective changes in the future.

3. **Scenario Modeling**: With the help of financial tools, you may simulate various events, such as fluctuations in rental income, interest rates, or expenses, in order to determine how they will affect cash flow and return on investment.

- Scenario modeling enables you to foresee future risks and possibilities, resulting in wiser investment decisions.

4. **Comparative Analysis**: distinct financial tools may perform comparative analysis, which compares distinct qualities side by side using different financial indicators.

- With the help of this function, you can quickly assess and contrast various investment options.

5. **Risk Assessment**: By examining elements like vacancy rates, market stability, and prospective economic downturns, financial software can assist in assessing the risks related to a certain investment.

- By recognizing and measuring risks, you can choose investments that take them into account.

6. **Portfolio Management**: By tracking performance, keeping an eye on cash flow, and assessing total returns, financial tools help you manage your real estate portfolio.

- They make the process of managing your portfolio more efficient and make sure that your assets match your risk tolerance and financial objectives.

7. **Data Visualization**: Many financial applications provide data visualization features, which exhibit financial data in straightforward charts and graphs.

- Visual representations facilitate decision-making by making it easier to spot trends and patterns.

8. **Investment Forecasting**: Based on historical data and anticipated market conditions, financial software may calculate future cash flow and ROI.

- Making long-term investment planning is made easier with the aid of investment forecasting.

You may invest in real estate with more knowledge by using financial software and tools, which can also save you time by eliminating the need for manual calculations and give you a deeper understanding of potential prospects. To supplement the outcomes of these tools with your knowledge and comprehension of the real estate market, it is crucial to employ trustworthy and reputable tools. The human element and skill are still essential for good decision-making, despite the fact that financial instruments are valuable resources. Let's use knowledge and technology to open the door to real estate wealth.

Chapter 4

Navigating Legal and Regulatory Aspects

Understanding real estate laws and regulations that affect investments

Any real estate investor must be aware of the laws and rules governing investments in real estate. These rules and laws are in place to safeguard both buyers and sellers, guarantee ethical behavior, and preserve the integrity of the real estate market. Here are some crucial points to think about:

1. **Property Ownership and Transfer**: Real estate laws regulate the establishment and transfer of property ownership. It is crucial to comprehend how title deeds, deeds of trust, and other legal documents are created.

Knowing the pertinent regulations in your area is essential because different jurisdictions may have unique requirements for property transfers.

2. Zoning and Land Use Regulations: Zoning rules control the use of properties in particular locations. To guarantee that you adhere to the approved land uses, familiarize yourself with the zoning laws.

- Look for any land use changes, building height limitations, or other restrictions that can affect your investment plans.

3. Contract Law and Disclosure Requirements:
- Real estate transactions involve various contracts, such as purchase agreements and lease agreements. Understanding the terms and conditions within these contracts is vital.

- Sellers are often required to disclose certain property defects or issues that may affect its value. Complying with disclosure requirements helps maintain transparency during the transaction.

4. **Landlord-Tenant Laws**:

- If you plan to become a landlord, it's essential to know landlord-tenant laws in your area. These laws govern rental agreements, eviction procedures, security deposits, and tenant rights.

- Complying with these laws ensures a smooth and legal landlord-tenant relationship.

5. **Fair Housing Laws**:

- Fair housing laws prohibit discrimination based on race, color, religion, sex, national origin, disability, or familial status. It's crucial to follow these laws when advertising rental properties and selecting tenants.

- Adhering to fair housing practices promotes equal opportunities for all potential renters.

6. **Environmental Regulations**:

- Environmental regulations may impact properties with potential environmental hazards. Understanding these regulations helps you assess the property's environmental risk.

- Factors such as hazardous substances, wetlands, and endangered species habitat may affect your investment decisions.

7. **Taxation and IRS Rules**:
- Real estate investment taxation can be complex. Understanding tax implications for rental income, capital gains, and depreciation is essential for maximizing returns.

- Utilizing tax strategies like 1031 exchanges can provide tax-deferred benefits.

To gain a comprehensive understanding of real estate laws and regulations, consider consulting with a real estate attorney or experienced real estate professionals. Compliance with these laws not only protects your investments but also establishes a foundation for ethical and successful real estate practices. Stay informed and proactive to navigate the legal aspects of real estate investing with confidence.

Exploring tax implications and strategies for maximizing returns.

Exploring tax implications and employing strategies to maximize returns is essential for successful real estate investing. Understanding how taxes impact your real estate investments can help you optimize your returns and minimize tax liabilities. Here are some tax considerations and strategies to explore:

1. **Rental Income Taxation**:
   - Rental income is generally taxable at your applicable income tax rate. Deduct eligible rental property expenses, such as property management fees, maintenance

costs, insurance, and property taxes, to reduce your taxable rental income.

- Keep accurate records of all income and expenses related to your rental property to facilitate tax reporting.

2. **Depreciation**:
- Depreciation is a valuable tax deduction that allows you to write off the cost of your investment property over its useful life.

- Residential properties can be depreciated over 27.5 years, while commercial properties can be depreciated over 39 years.

- Depreciation can significantly reduce your taxable income, providing additional cash flow and potential tax savings.

3. **1031 Exchanges**:
- Utilize a 1031 exchange to defer capital gains taxes when selling one investment property and acquiring a like-kind property.

- By reinvesting the proceeds from the sale into another property within specific timeframes, you can defer paying capital gains taxes until a future sale.

4. **Real Estate Investment Trusts (REITs)**:

- Consider investing in REITs, which are companies that own and manage income-generating real estate properties.

- REITs often offer tax advantages, as they distribute at least 90% of their taxable income to shareholders in the form of dividends, which are generally taxed at a lower rate.

5. **Passive Activity Loss Rules**:

- Real estate investments are often considered passive activities for tax purposes.

- Passive losses from rental properties may be limited based on your overall income. However, you may be able to offset passive losses against other passive income or carry them forward to future years.

6. Qualified Business Income Deduction (QBI):

- If you operate your real estate investments as a pass-through entity, such as an LLC or partnership, you may be eligible for the QBI deduction.

- The QBI deduction allows qualifying businesses to deduct up to 20% of their qualified business income, subject to certain limitations.

7. Tax Planning and Professional Advice:

- Regularly review your real estate investment tax strategy with a qualified tax professional to identify opportunities for optimization.

- A tax professional can help you navigate complex tax laws, plan for upcoming tax events, and make informed decisions to maximize your tax benefits.

By exploring tax implications and implementing effective tax strategies, you can enhance your real estate investment returns and increase your overall profitability. Remember, tax laws are subject to change, so staying informed and seeking professional advice are critical components of successful tax planning. With a well-executed tax strategy, you can unlock the full potential of your real estate investment journey.

Tips for conducting due diligence and avoiding legal pitfalls

Making informed decisions and avoiding potential legal hazards need extensive due diligence when investing in real estate. Here are some excellent advice for successfully completing due diligence:

1. **Verify Property Information**:
   - Obtain accurate and up-to-date property information, including title deeds, surveys, and any encumbrances on the property.

- Confirm the property's legal description and boundaries to avoid boundary disputes in the future.

2. **Review Financial Records**:
- Examine financial records, including income statements, rent rolls, and operating expenses.

- Assess the property's historical financial performance to gauge its profitability and potential for future returns.

3. **Assess Property Condition**:
- Conduct a thorough property inspection to identify any structural issues, maintenance needs, or potential hazards.

- Understanding the property's condition helps you estimate repair costs and negotiate the purchase price.

4. **Research Market Conditions**:
- Analyze the local real estate market and economic trends to gauge the property's potential for appreciation and rental demand.

- Being aware of market conditions helps you make informed decisions about the property's long-term viability.

5. **Check Zoning and Land Use**:
- Confirm the property's zoning and land use regulations to ensure it aligns with your intended use or investment strategy.

- Verify any restrictions or limitations that may impact your plans for the property.

6. **Investigate Tenancy and Lease Agreements**:
- If the property has existing tenants, review lease agreements and rental histories.

- Understand tenant rights and obligations to ensure a smooth transition if you plan to take over as the landlord.

7. **Look into Environmental Concerns**:
- Check for any potential environmental hazards or contamination on the property.

- Conduct environmental assessments if necessary, especially if the property was previously used for industrial or hazardous activities.

8. **Consult Professionals**:
- Seek guidance from real estate attorneys, property inspectors, and other professionals to ensure a comprehensive due diligence process.

- Professional advice can help you identify potential risks and address legal complexities.

9. **Review Legal and Regulatory Compliance**:
- Ensure the property complies with all relevant local, state, and federal laws and regulations.

- Check for any outstanding code violations or liens that may affect the property's marketability.

10. **Secure Appropriate Insurance Coverage**:

- Obtain appropriate property insurance coverage to protect your investment from unforeseen events and liabilities.

- Consult with insurance experts to ensure you have adequate coverage.

You can reduce your risk of running into legal snags and making judgments that are in line with your investing objectives by carefully observing these suggestions and performing thorough due research. Keep in mind that conducting due diligence is a continuous process throughout the real estate investment process, and that being proactive and thorough is the key to success. Let's move forward cautiously and confidently build the route to real estate wealth.

Chapter 5

Effective Property Management and Maintenance

The importance of effective property management in sustaining long-term profitability

Maintaining long-term profitability in real estate investing requires effective property management. It contributes to maximizing returns and asset appreciation and forms the basis of a successful investment strategy. Here are some reasons why managing a property effectively is so crucial:

1. **Tenant Retention and Reduced Vacancy**: A capable property management team places a strong emphasis on tenant

satisfaction, immediately handling requests and maintenance issues.

- Happy renters are more likely to have their leases renewed, which lowers vacancy rates and ensures a consistent flow of rental money.

2. **Timely Rent Collection**: By ensuring that rent is paid on time, property managers reduce the chance of delinquencies and increase cash flow.

Rent collection that is consistent over time helps to maintain a steady cash stream, which is essential for long-term profitability.

3. **Maintenance and repairs that are economical**:
- Proactive maintenance is a key component of effective property management, which helps to spot problems early and resolve them.

- Quick fixes maximize cost effectiveness by preventing small issues from becoming more serious and expensive repairs.

4. **Adherence to Regulations and Legal Obligations**: Property managers make sure that your investment properties follow municipal ordinances, construction rules, and safety requirements.

- Adherence to rules reduces legal risk and potential liabilities, protecting your investment.

5. **Marketing and Tenant Screening**: Effective property managers utilize targeted marketing techniques to draw in dependable tenants.

- Strict screening procedures for tenants aid in the selection of obedient tenants, lowering the possibility of late rent payments and property damage.

6. **Strategic Decision-Making**: - To make wise choices, property managers who

are effective in their jobs use data-driven insights and market expertise.

- They might suggest making changes to the rent, making improvements to the property, or taking other actions to improve the efficiency and profitability of the rental.

7. **Professional Experience and Time Management**: - Property management calls for specific training and experience in a range of fields, including law, finance, and tenant relations.

- Hiring a professional property management company frees up your time so you may concentrate on other investment options and strategic planning.

8. **Property Preservation and Value Enhancement**: - Careful property management maintains the property's structural integrity and visual attractiveness.

- Properties that are kept up well preserve their worth over time and even rise in value, which boosts overall profitability.

Maintaining long-term success in real estate investing requires effective property management. It makes sure tenants are happy, cuts down on vacant spaces, improves cash flow, and raises the value of the property. You set yourself up for ongoing success and wealth in the fast-paced real estate market by committing your investments to a capable property management company. Let's put a high priority on efficient property management to maximize the potential of our real estate wealth.

Tips for selecting reliable property managers and maintaining properties for maximum value

Successful real estate investing requires careful consideration when choosing a property manager and maintaining assets to maximize value. You may discover reputable property managers with the help of the following helpful hints, which will also help you make sure your properties maintain their value over time:

Tips for Selecting Reliable Property Managers:

1. Conduct a Comprehensive Search: Look into local property management firms and individual property managers. Seek out experts with a history of success who have experience.

2. Verify References and Reviews: - Request references from other property owners who have utilized the services of the prospective property management or organization.

- Consult online reviews and customer feedback to learn about other people's opinions.

3. Consider Specialization and Expertise: Opt for a property manager with experience in looking after properties that are similar to yours. Different property categories call for various management techniques.

4. Verify Licensing and Credentials: - Make sure the property manager has the licenses and credentials necessary to operate in accordance with local laws.

- A further sign of a professional's dedication is membership in organizations like the National Association of Residential Property Managers (NARPM), which is a professional association.

5. Communication and Responsiveness: - Look for property managers who communicate clearly and answer questions and concerns right away.

- For a positive landlord-tenant relationship, accessibility and clear lines of communication are crucial.

6. Understanding of Local legislation and Regulations: - Verify that the property management is informed about neighborhood fair housing legislation, landlord-tenant laws, and rental regulations.

- It's essential to follow the law in order to prevent future legal problems.

Tips for Maintaining Properties for Maximum Value

1. Regular Property Inspections: - Conduct routine property inspections to spot possible areas for improvement, maintenance needs, and safety issues.

- Resolve any maintenance problems right away to stop them from getting worse.

2. Preventive Maintenance: - Put preventive maintenance procedures in place to maintain the property's condition and avert costly repairs.

- Plan routine maintenance for the electrical, plumbing, and HVAC systems.

3. Invest in High-Quality Materials and Workmanship: - For repairs and improvements, use top-notch materials and use qualified contractors.

- Investing in quality increases tenant satisfaction and ensures the durability of renovations.

4. Keep Up with Market Trends: - Keep abreast of market developments and tenant preferences to make well-informed decisions about improvements and extras for the property.

5. Energy Efficiency Upgrades: - Put in place energy-saving measures to cut down on utility bills and draw in environmentally minded tenants.

- Give programmable thermostats, LED lights, and energy-saving appliances some thought.

Maintain open lines of communication with tenants and respond to their issues quickly.

Building positive tenant relations can lead to higher tenant retention and reduced turnover costs

Developing good tenant relationships is unquestionably an important aspect of real estate investing that can result in increased tenant retention and lower turnover expenses. Here are some reasons why maintaining good tenant relations is crucial to maintaining a successful rental property:

1. **Greater Tenant Satisfaction**: Tenants are more likely to be happy with their living situation when they have positive interactions with the landlord and property management.

 - Satisfied renters are more likely to renew their leases and stay for a longer period of time, which lowers turnover.

2. **Reduced Vacancy Rates**: Low vacancy rates are a direct result of high tenant retention. Long-term profitability is increased by fewer empty units since they generate constant and reliable rental income.

 - Less vacancies also mean lower marketing, advertising, and turnover-related costs.

3. **Lower Turnover expenditures**: - Turnover expenditures, such as those for cleaning, repairs, repainting, advertising, and tenant screening, can be substantial.

Positive tenant interactions reduce the chance of turnover, which lowers these costs and maintains the profitability of your investment.

4. **Referrals and Reputation**: - Reliable and responsible tenants are more likely to be attracted to your property by satisfied tenants, who are more likely to recommend it to their friends and family.

- Quality tenants are drawn to a company with a good reputation, which facilitates tenant screening and lowers the likelihood of dealing with problematic tenants.

5. **On-Time Rent Payments**: Good tenant relationships frequently result in higher rent collection rates.

- Tenants who get along well with the owner or manager are more likely to pay their rent on time, maintaining a consistent stream of income.

6. **Fewer Maintenance Issues**: Tenants who experience respect and value are more

likely to report maintenance issues right away.

 - Responding to maintenance requests right away not only ensures tenant satisfaction but also stops minor difficulties from becoming serious and expensive concerns.

7. **Increased Property Maintenance**: Tenants who get along well with the landlord or property manager are more inclined to maintain the property.

 - Less use and abuse on the property results in it lasting longer and maintaining its value.

An ideal situation for both landlords and tenants is one in which there are good tenant relations. You may improve the quality of living conditions for tenants, raise tenant satisfaction, and lower the costs related to eviction by encouraging a polite and helpful landlord-tenant relationship. The ongoing success and profitability of your real estate investment are ultimately a result of these efforts, which also result in improved tenant retention rates and lower vacancy rates. Let's place a higher priority on fostering good tenant relationships so that we can enjoy a well-kept and successful rental property.

Chapter 6

Adapting to Market Changes and Real Estate Cycles

Understanding the cyclical nature of the real estate market and how to adapt to changes

Successful real estate investing requires an understanding of the market's cyclical nature. Real estate markets experience regular expansion, peak, contraction, and trough cycles that are driven by macroeconomic forces and market dynamics. Here are some tips for adjusting to changes in the real estate market:

1. **Recognize Market Indicators**: - Keep up with important market indicators, such as real estate costs, supply levels, and sales volume.

- Keeping an eye on economic indices like GDP growth, unemployment rates, and interest rates can also give you important clues about how the real estate market is trending.

2. **Examine Past Trends**: Research past real estate cycles in your target markets to spot trends and foresee future developments.

- Analyzing historical trends might help you spot market peaks and troughs.

3. **Be Flexible and Agile**: - Acknowledge that market circumstances can change quickly. Be ready to modify your investing plan and timetable if necessary.

- Being nimble and adaptable enables you to take advantage of opportunities and safeguard your investments during all stages of the real estate cycle.

4. **Diversify Your Portfolio**: Reducing risk requires portfolio diversification. To

distribute risk throughout your portfolio, make investments in a variety of property kinds, regions, and markets.

- Diversification enables you to withstand market or property sector downturns.

5. **Assess Your Investment Horizon**: When making choices, take into account your investment horizon and risk tolerance.

- While long-term investors might put stability and revenue creation first, short-term investors might concentrate on properties with quick turnaround possibilities.

6. **Put Cash Flow First**: When making investments, especially in times of economic uncertainty, put cash flow first.

- Properties with positive cash flow offer stability and can aid in defraying operational costs during market downturns.

7. **Stay Educated and Informed**: - Keep yourself up to date on the real estate market, broader economic trends, and legislative developments.

- Go to industry gatherings, sign up for networking organizations, and keep tabs on the market through reliable sources.

8. **Consult with Experts**: - Ask knowledgeable real estate agents, economists, and financial consultants for their opinions.

- Consulting professionals can offer helpful vantage points and insights to successfully handle market shifts.

9. **Reduce Risks**: Take into account risk management techniques, such as insurance coverage and long-term financing, to safeguard your capital from unforeseen occurrences.

10. **Patience and a Long-Term View**: Recognize that real estate investing is a long-term endeavor. Be patient and abstain

from forming snap judgments based on transient market swings.

- Pay attention to the potential and worth of your real estate holdings in the long run.

Real estate market changes necessitate a combination of market expertise, strategic thinking, and risk management. You may position yourself for success and take advantage of possibilities in the always changing real estate market by maintaining your knowledge, being adaptable, and coordinating your investment choices with market cycles. On our path to real estate wealth, let's accept the market's cyclical nature and make wise decisions.

Strategies for mitigating risks during market downturns

Protecting your real estate interests and navigating economic hardships require risk mitigation during market downturns. Here are some practical tips to assist you in navigating market downturns:

1. **Build Cash Reserves**: - Keep enough cash on hand to meet operating expenditures, mortgage payments, and unforeseen bills in times of economic depression.

- A sizeable cash reserve acts as a safety net and guarantees that you can maintain your properties even during times of poor cash flow.

2. **Focus on Cash Flow**: - Give cash flow-positive properties a priority that provide enough rental income to pay for costs and debt commitments.

Strong cash flow properties are more resilient during market downturns, lowering financial stress.

3. **Long-Term Financing**: Take into account getting long-term, fixed-rate financing for your homes.

- During times of economic uncertainty, locking in a favorable interest rate shields you from prospective hikes.

4. **Diversification**: Spread out the properties in your real estate portfolio among various property types and geographical regions.

- Diversifying your investments can help your portfolio as a whole by reducing the overall impact of market downturns.

5. **Staggered Lease Expirations**: - Stagger your renters' lease expirations to prevent a lot of vacancies occurring at once.

This strategy assists in preserving a consistent rental income stream even during a downturn.

6. **Renegotiate Expenses**: - To save costs during market downturns, renegotiate service provider contracts.

- Look for ways to save money on utilities, property management, and upkeep.

7. **Communicate with Tenants**: - In difficult economic times, keep lines of contact with your tenants open and honest.

- Collaborate with them to address issues and, where needed, grant reasonable requests.

8. **Renovate and Improve**: If you want to increase the charm and value of your homes, think about performing strategic renovations or enhancements.

- Making improvements can draw in reputable tenants and possibly support higher rents.

9. **Monitor Market Trends**: - Keep up with market and economic data to gauge the depth and length of the recession.

- Understanding the state of the market can help you make wise judgments regarding your properties.

10. **Reevaluate Investment Strategies**:
- Reevaluate your investment strategy and modify it as necessary to conform to the circumstances of the present market.

- Determine the best course of action depending on your financial objectives and risk tolerance, whether to buy, hold, or sell.

You may reduce risks during market downturns and maintain stability in your real estate assets by putting these measures into practice. You can manage difficult economic circumstances and put yourself in a position for long-term success in the real estate market by being proactive and well-prepared. Let's maintain our fortitude and lay a strong foundation for real estate wealth in the face of any economic downturn.

Identifying emerging market opportunities and capitalizing on upswings

A crucial component of successful real estate investing is spotting developing market possibilities and taking advantage of upswings. Here are some practical tips to aid you in spotting new chances and capitalizing on market upswings:

1. **Market Research and Analysis**: - Conduct in-depth market research to pinpoint sectors with significant room for expansion.

   - Examine a variety of elements that affect real estate demand, including economic indicators, demographic trends, employment growth, infrastructural improvements, and others.

2. **Track Demographic Changes**: - Keep an eye on demographic changes and shifting buyer or renter preferences.

   - Locations where young professionals, families, or retirees are moving in may offer lucrative investment options.

3. Follow Urban Development Plans: - Keep up with regional government activities and urban development plans.

   - Investments near planned infrastructure upgrades or rehabilitation projects frequently see a rise in demand and value.

Search for markets or communities that are undervalued but have the potential to expand and undergo good transformation.

   - Making an investment in these sectors before the upswing can result in large rewards.

5. Network with Local Experts: - Create connections with real estate brokers, property managers, and other local professionals that have in-depth market expertise.

   - These linkages may offer insightful information about new prospects and trends.

6. **Follow Industry and Technology Trends**: - Keep abreast of business and technical developments that could have an impact on the real estate market.

- Demand for particular property types or locations might be sparked by developing industries or technologies.

Target emerging asset classes by investing in projects that include co-living areas, senior living communities, or mixed-use buildings.

- These cutting-edge property kinds can meet changing consumer wants and provide alluring profits.

8. **Act Quickly When Market Conditions Change**: - Be prepared to take advantage of opportunities when market conditions change in your favor.

- You can profit from upswings by having financial reserves and a clearly defined investment strategy.

9. **Profit from Seller's Markets**: You may be able to sell homes for more money when there is a seller's market, where demand outweighs supply.

- Take advantage of the current market's favorable conditions to increase your investment returns.

Use metrics that are future-focused.
- Base your investment choices on indicators that are looking ahead, such as projected population increase and employment prospects.

- Assessing potential for the future might offer you an advantage when spotting chances in developing markets.

By using these techniques, you may spot emerging market possibilities and put yourself in a position to profit from real estate market upswings. Making wise investments that result in long-term success and real estate wealth requires being proactive and knowledgeable. In order to succeed in the real estate industry, let's embrace the power of foresight and seize presenting possibilities.

Conclusion

At the end of the day, "Real Estate Riches: The Unlocking of the Codes to Successful Investments" has taken us on an insightful tour through the world of real estate investing. The fundamental ideas, methods, and approaches required to succeed and grow in this exciting and gratifying area have been covered in detail.

We examined the complexities of comprehending the real estate market in this book, as well as ways to identify significant factors and potential investment opportunities. In order to make wise decisions in any economic environment, we learnt to evaluate market trends and potential hazards.

We set out to develop a sound investment plan that was appropriate for our level of risk tolerance and financial resources, putting a strong emphasis on the value of having specific investment goals and objectives. We adopted the technique of managing risk and return in our financial pursuits after learning about the value of diversification and portfolio management.

We were able to carefully appraise possible properties by mastering financial analysis, weighing important factors including cash flow, cap rates, and ROI. We enabled ourselves to confidently make wise investment decisions by arming ourselves with financial tools and software.

We learned about the rules and tax repercussions that affect our investments through navigating legal and regulatory concerns. We picked up helpful pointers for completing due diligence, avoiding legal snares, and maximizing tax techniques for returns.

In order to fully comprehend their crucial responsibilities in upholding long-term profitability, we further investigated the area of efficient property management and upkeep. Our success became largely dependent on fostering good tenant relationships and establishing economical maintenance procedures.

Understanding the real estate market's cyclical nature and how to adjust to changes gave us the resiliency we needed to succeed in a field that was constantly changing. We took advantage of new market chances and discovered how to profit from upswings, seizing the chance to make significant gains.

Let's take the knowledge we've received from "Real Estate Riches" with us as we get to the end of our enlightening journey and put it to use right away. We now have the secrets to profitable real estate investments, and armed with this information and these tactics, we are prepared to start along the road to success.

May we all manage the real estate market with a commitment to quality, a vision for progress, and the knowledge that success is based on good ideas and forward-thinking tactics.

It's important to keep in mind that the real estate market is a place of limitless opportunity. By being diligent, flexible, and foresighted, we may find our own unique version of "Real Estate Riches" and leave a legacy of wealth for both ourselves and future generations.

It is now time to put our knowledge to use, face the difficulties ahead, and take advantage of the chances presented by the constantly changing real estate investing environment. Let's go out on this adventure with self-assurance, tenacity, and a desire to carve out our own paths to success in the alluring world of real estate. I look forward to the path ahead and seeing our real estate goals come true.

About Author

Michael Lawson is a recognized author, experienced investor, and real estate specialist who has a love for encouraging people to succeed financially through real estate investing. Michael has over 20 years of expertise in the business and is well-known among investors, real estate experts, and aspiring business owners alike.

Michael comes from a family of real estate lovers, thus his foray into the world of real estate started when he was very young, sparking a passion for the business of wise investing that has lasted his entire life. He soon developed his skills, generating profitable investments that laid the groundwork for his flourishing career. He had a strong eye for market patterns and a cunning understanding of financial research.

When Michael decided to share the secrets of real estate wealth with readers all over the world, he turned from a successful investor to a highly sought-after author. He did this out of a genuine desire to share his wisdom and concepts. His best-selling book, "Real Estate Riches: The Unlocking of the Codes to Successful Investments," serves as a comprehensive guide that provides readers with a road map for navigating the difficult real estate investing industry.

The approachability of Michael Lawson's writing style and his aptitude for reducing complicated ideas to workable solutions are both well-known qualities. His writing is compelling to readers of all skill levels, whether he is describing financial research or highlighting the value of efficient property management.

In addition to writing, Michael actively imparts his knowledge through workshops, speaking engagements, and mentorship initiatives. His commitment to empowering others has established him as a motivational speaker, encouraging aspirant investors to make risky moves for financial independence.

As a thought leader in the real estate sector, Michael keeps up with changing market conditions, staying ahead of new trends and seizing opportunities. In their quest for real estate success, his readers are certain to receive the most current and pertinent information because of his dedication to staying at the forefront of the business.

Michael Lawson is committed to assisting others in accomplishing their financial objectives and has a strong belief in the transforming power of real estate investing. He has cemented his position as one of the most prominent voices in the real estate industry by having a tremendous impact on the lives of countless people.

When Michael isn't researching new investment options or writing informative blog posts, he likes to spend time with his family, indulge in his passion of travel, and give to organizations that promote affordable housing and neighborhood improvement.

Michael Lawson is a source of knowledge and motivation for individuals looking for a dependable mentor in their quest for real estate wealth because of his experience and dedication to excellence. Through his efforts, he continues to open doors for other investors to realize the real estate market's potential and leave a legacy of financial success.